Ants

Vivian French

OXFORD
UNIVERSITY PRESS

OXFORD
UNIVERSITY PRESS

Great Clarendon Street, Oxford, OX2 6DP, United Kingdom

Oxford University Press is a department of the University of Oxford. It furthers the University's objective of excellence in research, scholarship, and education by publishing worldwide. Oxford is a registered trade mark of Oxford University Press in the UK and in certain other countries

Text © Vivian French 2016

Illustrations © Madison Mastrangelo 2016

Inside cover notes written by Catherine Baker

The moral rights of the author have been asserted

First published 2016

All rights reserved. No part of this publication may be reproduced, stored in a retrieval system, or transmitted, in any form or by any means, without the prior permission in writing of Oxford University Press, or as expressly permitted by law, by licence or under terms agreed with the appropriate reprographics rights organization. Enquiries concerning reproduction outside the scope of the above should be sent to the Rights Department, Oxford University Press, at the address above.

You must not circulate this work in any other form and you must impose this same condition on any acquirer

British Library Cataloguing in Publication Data
Data available

ISBN: 978-0-19-837111-3

10 9 8 7 6 5 4 3 2 1

Paper used in the production of this book is a natural, recyclable product made from wood grown in sustainable forests. The manufacturing process conforms to the environmental regulations of the country of origin.

Printed in China by Golden Cup

Acknowledgements

Series Editor: Nikki Gamble

The publisher would like to thank the following for permission to reproduce photographs:

P1: Redmond Durrell/Alamy Stock Photo; All other images by Shutterstock.

Contents

The Colony 6

Jobs 7

Babies 8

Strength 10

Food 11

Big and Small 14

Glossary and Index 16

My little brother Sam loved watching ants.

"Look!" Sam said. "Beetles!"

"Those are ants," I said. "Ants are clever."

"Why?" Sam asked.

"Can you see those feelers on its head?" I said. "Those are **antennae**. Ants use them to tell each other about food and danger!"

"Ants look after each other," I said. "They live in a group, just like a big family! The group is called a **colony**."

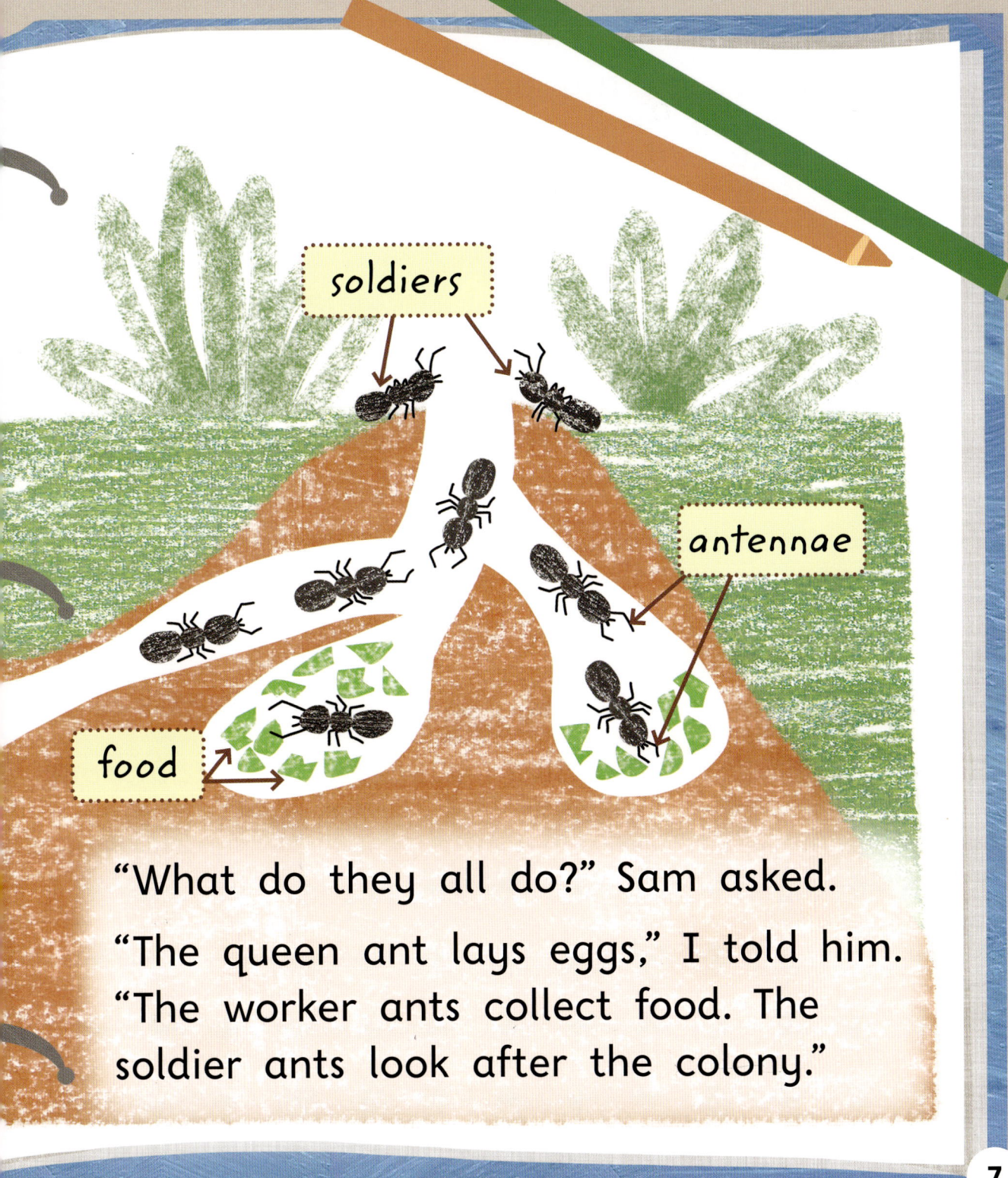

"What do they all do?" Sam asked.

"The queen ant lays eggs," I told him. "The worker ants collect food. The soldier ants look after the colony."

Sam looked at my picture.
"What are ant babies like?" he asked.

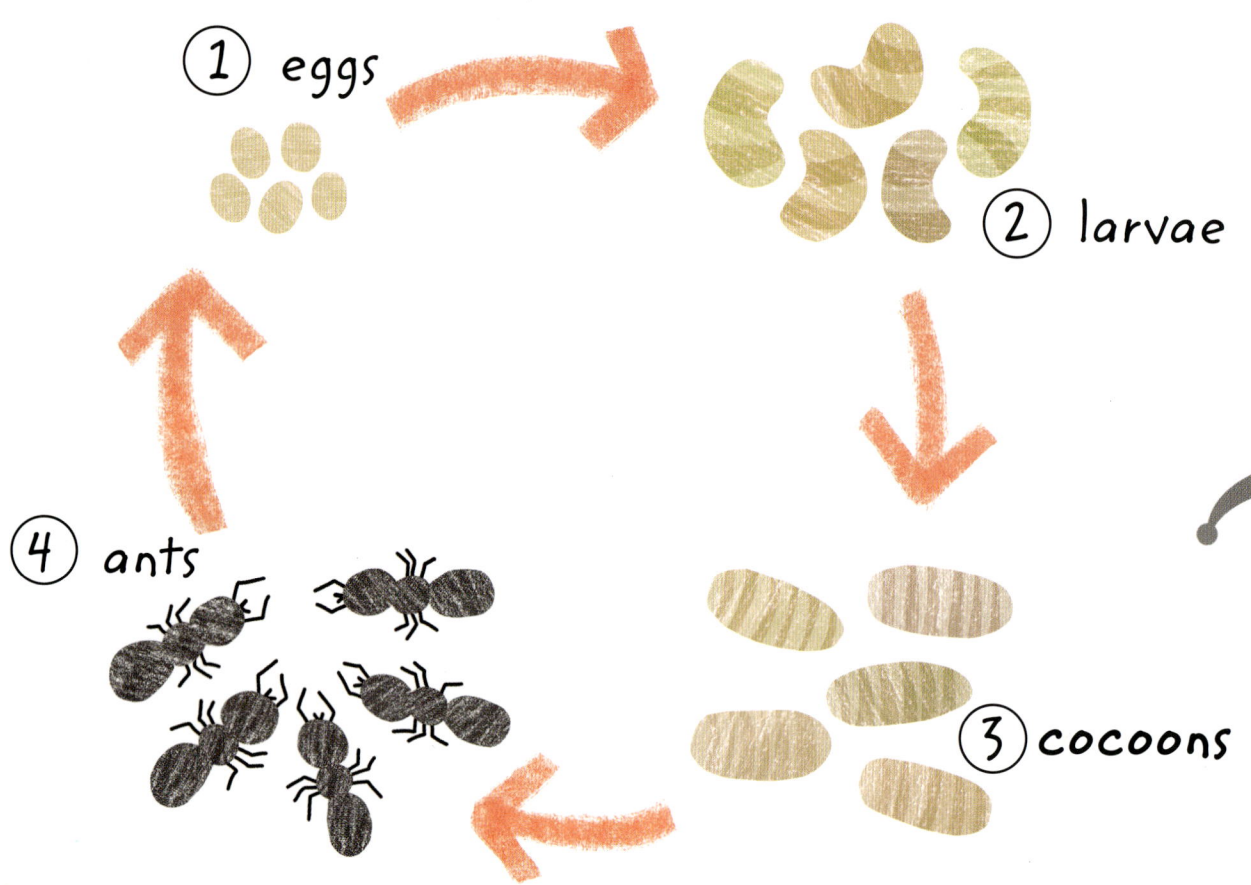

"First, the queen lays some eggs," I told him. "The eggs hatch into larvae. Then the larvae make cocoons and turn into ants."

"Tell me about the soldier ants," said Sam. "Do they fight?"

"Yes," I said. "Sometimes they fight the ants from another colony."

"Did you know that ants are very strong?" I asked. "If Dad was as strong as an ant, he could carry a car!"

"What do ants eat?" Sam asked.
He liked eating.

"They eat almost anything!" I said.
"They like fruit, seeds and dead bugs.
And they love sugar!"

Sam frowned. "They might eat my cake!" he said.

"Well, people eat ants in some parts of the world!" I said.

I pointed at an ant. "Look how tiny it is. The biggest ants are longer than your thumb! They live in South America."

There are more than 12 000 different sorts of ant.

smallest = 1 millimetre

largest = 30 millimetres

Sam let an ant crawl over his hand. "I love ants ..." he said.

"That's good," I said. "Because there are lots and lots and lots of ants in the world!"

Glossary

antennae: long, thin feelers on an insect's head

cocoons: coverings that protect baby insects while they change into adults

colony: a group of animals that live and work together

larvae: tiny animals that hatch out of eggs and turn into insects

millimetre: a way of measuring how long something is

Index

antennae.. 5, 7
cocoons.... 8
colony...... 6, 7, 9
eggs 6, 7, 8
food 5, 7, 11–13
larvae....... 6, 8
queen....... 6, 7, 8
soldiers..... 7, 9
workers 6, 7